Ellen Garcia

Human personality. The Five Factor Trait Theory

GRIN Verlag

Bibliografische Information der Deutschen Nationalbibliothek:

Die Deutsche Bibliothek verzeichnet diese Publikation in der Deutschen National-bibliografie; detaillierte bibliografische Daten sind im Internet über http://dnb.d-nb.de/ abrufbar.

Imprint:

Copyright © 2013 GRIN Verlag GmbH
Druck und Bindung: Books on Demand GmbH, Norderstedt Germany
ISBN: 978-3-656-63783-7

This book at GRIN:

http://www.grin.com/en/e-book/271551/human-personality-the-five-factor-trait-theory

Big five:

1. Neuroticism
2. agreableness
3. extroversion - introversion
4. Openness
5. Conscientiousness

Trait Theory

Trait theory was developed from the concept of trait which simply describes the characteristic behavior of individuals thus their personality. Trait encompasses all aspects of how individuals perceive, believes and feels about things. This is what distinguishes individuals from one another. Trait theories are therefore concerned with understanding the differences in people's personality and establish the causes of these perceived differences. Although different theories have been developed by different people, they all base on the following assumptions: people genetically inherit traits from their biological parents; some traits are predominantly suited for leadership; and people who make good leaders have the correct if not sufficient combination of traits (Digman, 1990). It is through these assumptions that this theory has formed a good basis for selection of leaders thus a very important discipline in management. This essay therefore seeks to discuss 'five factor' trait theory highlighting some of the advantages and disadvantages of using such a theory to select leaders in the workforce.

Unlike the traditional psychological researches, contemporary psychological researchers in personality have managed to come up with a more comprehensive and empirical model for analyzing personality traits known as 'the five factor' or the 'big five' theory (Digman, 1990). The 'five factor' theory is a five factor model with broad categories of personality traits, each category having its distinct behavioral characteristics associated with them. Though the theory is new, the five factor model has proved to be one of the most practical and applicable model in studying human personality and has thus been accorded critical attention (Digman 1990)

The five factors

The 'big five' is a model of five factors including neuroticism, agreeableness, extroversion-introversion, openness and conscientiousness as discussed below (Ewen, 1998).

Extroversion-Introversion

Extroversion is a trait marked by pronounced interest in individuals outside world. Extroverts are very social, adventurous and have high confidence for establishing the unknown (Ewen, 1998). Character traits associated with extroversion include talkativeness, assertiveness, excitability, sociability, and increased emotional expression. Extroverts are very outgoing and will always answer *'yes'* to any potential challenge.

Introversion is the complete opposite of extroversion. Introverts are more quiet, lack interest in the outside world, deliberate and have a low-key interaction level. Their lack of interaction in the social world has always been interpreted as a sign of depression or shyness but this is never the case. Introverts simply require more time to be on their own to recharge and needs very minimal levels of stimulation as opposed to extroverts (Ewen, 1998).

If this factor is used to select individuals for leadership positions, extroverts are better fit leaders than introverts since they can handle challenges, lead groups of people and have desire to explore the unknown.

Neuroticism

Neuroticism is also referred by some as emotional stability. In most cases, adjustment has been used instead of neuroticism as most scholars argue that the term neuroticism has a more inherent negative denotation as most people associate it with mental capacity as opposed to emotion (Digman, 1990). Ewen (1989) defines neuroticism as a *"dimension of personality defined by instability and high anxiety at one end vs. stability and low anxiety on the other end* (p. 290).

Individuals with high scores of neuroticism are usually associated with negative emotion feelings like anger, anxiety, or depression. Such individuals respond with intense and in emotionally abnormal way to events that are rather considered less threatening by most people. In other words individuals under this category are likely to interpret simple everyday situations as threatening or just minor frustrations as very difficult rendering them helpless (Ewen, 1989). Such people are always in a bad mood. Such high levels of emotional instability is likely to lower their neurotic ability to clearly think, make conscious decisions and cope with stress hence they can never make good leaders.

People with low scores of neuroticism on the other hand are less emotionally reactive and upset. They are calmer, less depressed, emotionally stable, and rarely suffer persistent negative feelings.

Agreeableness

Agreeableness as a dimension of personality is simply a measure of how compatible individuals are with others. It is a measure of social cooperation and harmony.

Agreeable individuals value friendship and are thus friendly, helpful, considerate, and generous and are more willing to trade their interests for others (McCrae and Costa, 1987). They have an optimistic perception of human nature. They hold the belief that people are principally honest, trustworthy and descent. This personality trait is positive especially for those seeking

2

popularity. Agreeableness is however dangerous in situation where one is required to make tough objective decisions. Such people can never make good scientists, solders or critics which require a tougher and objective approach thus fit for disagreeable individuals

Disagreeable individuals on the other hand are more egocentric. They are less concerned with the well being of others and are less likely to extend help to other people. They have a dangerous pessimistic view of human nature and are always suspicious, uncooperative and unfriendly (McCrae and Costa, 1987).

4. Conscientiousness

Conscientiousness as a personality dimension refers to how much an individual take others into consideration when making decisions. It is simply a factor which determines how well individuals manage, regulate and direct their impulses. Individuals who scores high on conscientiousness usually think of how their decisions will impact on the others. They are generally orderly, care about getting things done right, avoid troubles, arrive on time, and get their work done (McCrae and Costa, 1987). Conscientious individuals always strive to achieve high levels of success, and others regard them positively as reliable and intelligent. However extremely conscientious individuals are always workaholic and sometimes compulsive perfectionists. They are thus regarded as stuffy and boring to be around.

Unconscientious individuals on the other hand, have less desire for success, unreliable and are never time conscious but are never boring to be around hence very desirable for social interactions.

5. Openness

Openness as a personality dimension simply refers to how willing individuals are to adjust to new ideas (Ewen, 1989). Openness dimension simply differentiates creative and imaginative people from conventional and down to earth individuals. Individuals who score high in openness are appreciative of art, sensitive to beauty and intellectually curious. Psychologists compare them to closed people who are more aware of their feelings thus hold individualistic and unconventional beliefs.

On the other hand, people with low scores on openness are associated with narrow, common interests. They rather prefer straight forward, plain and obvious situations over the more complex, subtle and ambiguous. Ewen (1989) explains that such people are always hesitant to try new ways of doing things.

The Trait Approach to Leadership

The scientific study of the relationship between leadership and personality has been more focused on the personality traits of effective leaders. Trait theory uses the premise that people are born leaders thus leaders can never be created. Before any further discussion on this topic, let me first define the term leadership. Leadership can be defined simply as a characteristic that enables an individual to head and inspire a group of people towards realizing a common interest or goal. This therefore means that an effective leader should be able to always be on the front and lead by example.

Following this definition, trait theory is more focused on personality traits as denoted by the five factors previously discussed to separate incapable leaders from capable leaders. Personality traits such as intelligence, honesty, integrity, self-confidence, charisma, stress tolerance, high energy level, and task-relevant knowledge are associated with leaders (Bolden et al. 2003). However some of the empirical studies have proved this wrong stating that the 'common' leadership traits are actually not common to most leaders in the practical scenario thus questioning its applicability in selecting leaders in the workplace.

Advantages of Trait Approach to Leadership Selection

The trait theory is built on the conception that leaders have certain personality traits that make them different from any other person. This is in consistent with the notion we hold that leaders should be outstanding individuals who are able to perform extra-ordinary tasks. Based on this premise, any manager selecting leaders will look for outstanding characters thus end up with effective leaders in the workplace.

Besides, trait theory has been researched for many years giving it its credibility as a model for leadership selection. Although through field studies, it has emerged that certain characteristic traits are not common in all successful leaders, traits such as group task supportiveness, technical skill, task motivation, administrative skill, social skill, application to task, emotional control, intelligence, charisma, and friendliness have been found to be persistent with many successful leaders (Bolden et al, 2003), hence a good basis for any leadership selection.

Another significance of this theory in leadership studies is derived from how the leader component is highlighted in this theory. Although leadership is a whole discipline composing of leaders, subjects and situations, trait theory chooses to concentrate on leaders alone. By doing so, the theory has managed to generate a more understanding of how the leader and his personality relate to the leadership process. Through such immense knowledge leaders are able to clearly understand their role in leadership and how their personality is likely to affect their performance.

Lastly the trait theory has managed to provide a benchmark for personal evaluation. Traits of a good leader are elaborately outlined in this theory hence an individual can easily identify the traits he need to possess if he has ambitions of being a leader. Personality assessment procedures can be used during leadership selection to ensure the best leaders are selected.

Disadvantages of Trait Approach to Leadership

Trait theory of leadership was developed on the premise that certain personality characteristics are associated with successful leadership and is thus common in all leaders. Studies have however proved that these characteristics (high energy level and intelligence) are not actual common in all successful leaders as some leaders did not portray them despite their success (Ewen, 1998). It is therefore more apparent that the fact that an individual does not posses certain traits cannot be a reason enough to be disqualified in as a leader. Besides, the theory has failed to come up with a definitive list of personality traits to be associated with leadership. The list of leadership traits is endless and can be confusing. This only means that a universal leadership trait does not exist. If such generalized characteristics are used when selecting leaders in the workforce, it is likely that they might either end up with poor leaders or better still leave out people who would otherwise make good leaders.

Another shortcoming of this theory is the fact that it deliberately failed to take situations into account. Leadership traits are more influenced by the situation at hand. People who possess certain traits that make them effective leaders in a particular situation may not be effective in another situation. Moreover, some people may simply have traits that make them potential leaders but may not be able to sustain such traits over time. If such leaders are selected in to the workplace, they are likely to fail in the administration of their duties.

The massive research on this subject has only led to subjectivity in the identification of leadership traits. What one author may perceive as effective leadership traits may not be the same for another author. This only means that even in recruitment situations, identification of leadership traits may be very subjective hence people who have good leadership traits may be left out if their traits were not in the criteria list.

Trait Approach to Leadership

Despite the many research on this subject, none has explored the relationship between leadership traits and leadership outcomes. The researches instead concentrate on the link between leadership traits and leadership emergence without even trying to establish how such traits have affected performance of other group members. A leader is supposed to lead and inspire members of the group to success. It is clear that an individual can never posses all the positive attributes of the five factors discussed earlier in this essay. It could be possible that just the one missing trait dimension is dangerous to other group members hence affects his general leadership outcome. Any organization who wants to select effective leaders should rather concentrate on documented results of how such leadership traits have impacted on the general outcome of groups and teams.

Lastly, the notion of trait theory that leaders are born not made is out of place. Such a notion dismisses any possibility of training. Leadership skills are learned and that is why we have management training programs. Poor leaders can be couched to be good leaders so long as they have the skills and good will. If leaders are selected merely on their traits we are likely to leave out people with the right expertise who could have otherwise been trained to be good leaders.

Conclusion

Trait theory is a five factor model that seeks to understand why individuals behave differently from one another. The theory is built on the premise that our external expressions are more influenced by internal factors. These factors can be summarized into five as; Extroversion-introversion, neuroticism, agreeableness, conscientiousness and openness. The theory believes that these factors define personality traits hence very important in leadership studies, the main notion being that leaders are born not made. With the massive research in this field it has both been appreciated and criticized as a mechanism for selecting leaders in the workplace. Despite its much criticism, trait theory has emerged as the best model for establishing and selecting potential leaders since it gives a benchmark against which individual traits can be evaluated.

References

Bolden, R. et al (2003): *A review of Leadership Theory and competency frame works.* Edited Version of a report for Chase Consulting and management Standards Centre. United Kingdom: Centre for Leadership Studies, University of Exeter.

Digman, J. M. (1990): Personality structure: Emergence of the five-factor model. *Annual Review of Psychology,* 41, 417-440.

Ewen, R. B. (1998): *Personality*: A topical approach. Mahweh, NJ: Erlbaum.

McCrae, R. & Costa, P (1987): Validation of the five-factor model of personality across instruments and observers. *Journal of Personality and Social Psychology, 52, 81-90.*

CPSIA information can be obtained
at www.ICGtesting.com
Printed in the USA
440968LV00007B/14

* 9 7 8 3 6 5 6 6 3 7 8 3 7 *